GW00858480

How NOT To Write
an App

Rodney D. Cambridge

Copyright © 2011 Rodney D. Cambridge

All rights reserved.

ISBN: 1463766858
ISBN-13: 978-1463766856

For everyone who persists.

CONTENTS

PREFACE

An interesting thing about Apple's Think Different marketing campaign was the apparent misdirection surrounding the intended target of the campaign. Conventional thinking assumed that the phrase *Think Different* was aimed at Apple's customers – that somehow, by purchasing Apple goods, you were thinking different and, by thinking different, you were a cut above the rest; no stuffy, boring, grey corporate products for you! By buying into Apple, you were challenging the status quo – and looking cool at the same time.

As with many things, though, all is not what it seems with this campaign; Steve Jobs (the Apple CEO for the un-initiated) is a master of misdirection. After leaving Apple in the mid 80's, he returned over ten years later to find a struggling company on the verge of bankruptcy. Jobs set about culling many product lines and projects that were not seen as core products. These included the Newton PDA who many see as the grandfather, if not the father, of the iPhone.

With a demoralized workforce, the Think Different campaign and slogan were put in place. But, while everyone assumed that they were aimed at customers, the truth is that Steve Jobs aimed the Think Different campaign at Apple employees. It was Steve's way of encouraging, inspiring, and re-energizing his workers to get back to the task at hand - to pull out every last stop and put their hearts and souls into producing the innovative, pioneering and cutting edge products that he knew were necessary to turn the faltering company around.

Sometimes, looking at something in a different way enables you to see things that, previously, you would have missed. That's why I decided to think differently with this ebook and approach it from a different viewpoint.

There are many books around that claim to show you how to write a blockbuster smartphone app that will bring you untold riches once the app goes on sale on Apple's iTunes App store, or one of its many rivals such as Google's Marketplace.

My original plan was to join the throng and write an ebook that showed how to write a 'successful' app that would make you rich – but then I realised something; even though I designed, developed and shipped a successful app that generates an additional monthly income, that app didn't make me a millionaire.

Yes – I made, and continue to make, a decent amount of money from it, but it's hardly 'give- up-your-day-job' stuff. So, in truth, I couldn't write an ebook showing *you* how to become a millionaire. This is where I believe the majority of those other ebooks fail; they're approaching this thing from the wrong direction.

So – rather than try to tell you how to become rich, this ebook aims to tell you how to minimize the potential of lucking out with your app.

NOTE: While my app writing experience is specific to Apple's iOS platform, the topics, ideas and advice contained within this ebook applies to apps from other platforms, too.

GENESIS

Back in 2008, shortly after Apple's App store went live, I decided it would be a good idea to write an iPhone app. I kept hearing stories about how some developer had written an app, posted it to the App store and, within the space of a couple of months, had become rich beyond his wildest dreams.

It sounded straightforward enough – so I thought I'd give it a go; I had nothing to lose, after all. After a bit of thinking, I came up with a unique app idea that I called *Top-Tens*. The app would show the user the top 10s of any category that they wanted to track – be it books, video games, apps, etc. The app would employ a *client-server* model where the top 10 lists would be updated on a regular basis on the 'back end' meaning that every time the user opened the app, the latest top 10s would be displayed as long as they had an Internet connection. I ran the idea by a few people and it was met with universal endorsement.

So – all systems go! I bought a Mac mini, (I needed a development machine, obviously). I bought some iPhone programming books; I bought some sandals, grew a beard and went to work. (I didn't actually do the last two on that list, but I thought it sounded funny).

Luckily, I've got a background in programming – so it didn't take me long to get my head around the inner workings of Apple's Software Development Kit (SDK) which allows you to create the apps.

Five months later, I had my first app in the store. Did it make me rich beyond my wildest dreams? In dollar terms, no it didn't. However, in terms of what I learned during the process, absolutely!

And so I thought I'd share the experience with you!

INTENDED AUDIENCE

This book is intended for anyone who is in the process of, or contemplating, writing a smartphone or tablet app for Apple's iPhone, iPad, or one of the many other mobile platforms available today, including Google's Android, Motorola's Xoom, Microsoft's Windows Mobile, etc.

Writing and delivering an app can be quite a daunting task with many bases that need covering, including research, design, development, marketing, technical support, and more.

If you are about to embark on the journey, and especially if you're a lone developer wearing the many hats mentioned above, this book is for you. This book is divided into Lessons. While each lesson can be taken and read as a standalone unit, it makes sense to read them in the logical order in which they're presented. In addition, some lessons build on, and refer to, previous lessons.

So if you're ready, let's get started.

LESSON 1: SO WHAT'S AN APP?

"I keep hearing about apps. Apps for this. Apps for that. Seems like there's an app for almost everything! But what actually are apps? And can I write one?"

Apps 101

First, let's get this straight. Apps are nothing new. Google's successful Apps suite of online services which include webmail, calendars, etc. first saw the light of day in 2002. However lately, the term has been hijacked by Apple's marketing machine and has become synonymous with the programs that run on Apple's iPhone and related devices. When we refer to apps in this ebook, we mean mobile apps in general. In other words, we're referring to apps that run on a wide variety of smartphones and tablet devices and not specifically iPhone apps, (unless we state otherwise).

Put simply, an app is a smartphone or tablet computer application that does something. As the shortened name implies, apps typically have less functionality than the 'grown up' applications that run on desktop computers or laptops. For example, an email app running on a smartphone might allow you to send and receive email (as you might expect) and even create folders so that you can move and organize your mail neatly, but it probably won't provide you with the advanced features found in a desktop email application such as rules and smart folders which enable you to organize your mail to an even greater degree.

So apps usually take the form of 'cut down' versions of the more mature desktop applications. And there are a number of reasons why:

• **Screen size** – apps running on a smartphone or tablet computer typically have much less screen real estate to play with than traditional computers. Because of this, it's not desirable (or indeed, possible) to squeeze the UI (User Interface) of a full application into a much smaller form factor. Another consequence of screen size is that, unlike traditional applications, apps running on smartphones typically tend to run *full screen*. That is, they don't run in windows that can be resized or moved about. Normally an app takes up the entire screen (and therefore, the focus) of the device it's running on.

• **Usage models** – the usage model of a program on a smartphone or tablet is very different than that of a traditional laptop or desktop computer. These so-called 'mobile' apps are normally used for very short periods of time. They're launched, maybe to check email or the weather, and then closed again shortly after, whereas 'proper' applications typically remain open and in use for hours at a time. Game apps are an exception, of course. Much like games on other platforms, these apps can be used for hours on end.

• **System resource** – smartphones and tablets typically have less system resources than traditional laptop or desktop computers. For example, a desktop computer may have 4 or even 8 GB of RAM, whereas a smartphone may only have RAM totalling 256 or 512MB. With much less available system memory, care must be taken when coding the app to ensure that it runs efficiently in low memory conditions. In addition, processors on mobile platforms are typically much less powerful than those available on most desktop machines, thereby restricting the types of apps that can be developed on these platforms. App developers should bear this in mind when deciding on a platform to develop for.

• **Cost** – as the majority of mobile apps provide a less complete feature set when compared to 'proper' applications, they normally cost much less. However feature set is only one aspect of an app's price. The *race to the bottom* where app developers find themselves forced into pricing their app cheaply in order to be competitive is another contributor. More on this later in the book.

The 80/20 Rule
Taking the above into account, apps generally tend to employ the 80/20 rule when this rule is applied to proper applications: For 80% of the time, only

20% of the functionality of an application is used. For example, if you've been using your Word processor today, you probably used the same features to format and produce your document as you did yesterday; maybe you included a table, or added some images. Common activities like these, which are performed by most users, make up some of the 20% of functionality that's used 80% of the time. However, slightly more obscure functions such as adding citations and tables of authorities probably won't.

So a smartphone or tablet app will pretty much always consist only of that 20% functionality that is used the majority of the time. The rest is simply not needed and therefore doesn't make the cut. Anyone planning to write a mobile app should bear the 80/20 rule in mind when deciding on the feature set for their app.

What types of apps are there?
There is a wide, and growing, spectrum of apps available. As mentioned above, the majority are 'cut down' or mobile apps, however some apps are 'Enterprise-class'. This means that the app is robust and full featured enough to be used in 'Enterprise' (or big business) environments. One of the most common Enterprise-class apps is email, and it's easy to see why; being able to pick up corporate email on your Android device is not only cool, but it's ultra-convenient too. Chances are, the app that 95% of readers of this ebook are thinking of writing will not be an Enterprise-class app, and so I won't spend any time discussing the security implications and the things that you need to put in place in order to deliver such an app; I'm saving that for my follow-up ebook.

When it comes to 'normal' mobile apps, there are vast differences. Some apps make farting noises – and some developers have become rich off of the back of that type of app. But it's been done now. So please, don't think you'll make a mint by writing and selling yet another farting app. It's just not going to happen. Got that? Farting apps stink! And you shouldn't be going anywhere near them.

Some apps are pretty cool, some are pretty useful, and some are pretty useless. Some apps are just pretty. And, of course, some apps are rather more aesthetically challenged. Either way, there are a lot of apps available in a lot of different genres. Here are some of the more popular types:

- Business
- Education
- Entertainment
- Finance
- Games
- Health & Fitness
- Lifestyle
- Medical
- Music
- Navigation
- News
- Photography
- Productivity
- Reference
- Social Networking
- Sport
- Travel
- Utilities

These are just top-level categories to give you an example; there are many more sub- categories available, all crammed with apps. App stores typically list and organise the apps they sell via these top-level categories.

What's an App store?
Before Apple introduced the iPhone back in 2007, the concept of an App store as we know it today didn't really exist. Prior to the iPhone, if you had a smartphone and you wanted to install a program onto it, you had to visit the software developer's website, purchase the program, download it to your computer, and then transfer it to your device. In the main, it was certainly not a bad experience, although compared to the App store model some areas could be improved. For example:

- 	**Impartial advice** – one of the great things about an App store is that you will find impartial ratings and reviews from other users for each of the apps on sale. This means that you're less likely to be swayed by the developer's bold, and sometimes misleading, copy that may be present on their own website or online store. Of course, some developers try to play the system by creating multiple accounts on the App store and posting glowing reviews of their app from these fake users. That's not a cool thing to do. Developers who do this and get found out will generally find their app removed from the App store. I love Karma.

• **Discovery** – a well designed App store will allow and encourage browsing by the user, in order to facilitate the discovery and purchasing of as many apps as possible. In contrast, visiting a sole developer's website to purchase a program provides zero discoverability of other apps from other genres, top seller lists, etc.

• **Choice** – when you visit the developer's website to purchase his new To-Do application, you only get one choice. Visiting an App store and browsing the apps in the Productivity section will typically highlight many To-Do apps, allowing you to compare the apps based on various criteria such as price, feature set, reviews, ratings, etc.

• **Standards** – a developer can create an app over a weekend and put it up for sale on his or her website with little, or no, checking for things such as compliancy with accepted UI or usability guidelines. In contrast some (not all) App stores are regulated. This means that for an app to reach the 'for sale' stage on the store, it must have passed a number of tests and conditions. While having guidelines such as these in place will help ensure that the apps you purchase from the store don't both suck and blow at the same time, be aware that some will *still* suck.

Should I sell my app through an App store?

Following on from the success of Apple's App store for its iPhone and other iOS devices, (iPod touch and iPad), many other companies have created their own app stores through which users of their devices can purchase apps. For example, Google have the Android Market which allows users of Android OS devices to obtain apps, Palm have the App Catalog, Microsoft has the Windows Marketplace, RIM has the BlackBerry App World, etc.

The concept of an App store where users can easily obtain apps is, therefore, well proven and so it makes sense that your app should be distributed in the same way. Indeed, with some platforms, the App store is the *only* officially sanctioned way to sell your app.

Normally, when you sell your app through an App store, the store takes a percentage of the sale price. For most stores, this is around 30%. So if your app is on sale for £1, every time you make a sale, you get 70p while the company running the store gets 30p. Simples.

Some people don't like the idea of giving away 30% of their hard-earned money, though. While you might think that this is a terrible deal, remember that simply having your app available for sale on the store can make it visible to literally millions of potential customers; For example, Apple's App store app comes pre-installed on every single iPhone, iPod touch or iPad sold by the company. That's a lot of opportunity for sales. Especially when you take into account sales figures made available after a lawsuit was instigated by Apple against Samsung in April, 2011. The details in the lawsuit show that as of March, 2011, Apple has sold more than 108 million iPhones, over 60 million iPod touches and over 19 million iPads. Exciting numbers!

Having your app hosted on an App store means that a good deal of marketing has already been undertaken for you. People know where to get your app from – and these people frequent the store on a regular basis. In addition, you don't have to pay additional server hosting fees, etc.

Contrast this with trying to sell the app straight from your own website with none of these benefits, and the 30% per sale actually starts sounding very reasonable!

What's a web app?

There are two main types of app: *Web apps* and *Native apps.*

Native apps are the most common type. A native app is an app that has been written using a software development kit (SDK) to run on a specific device. For example, a native iPhone app has been written to run on the iPhone's OS Operating System (OS) and needs to be able to 'see' the iPhone's hardware and firmware in order to run properly. If you attempt to run the app on another device it simply won't work because the other device will be running a different OS and will also have different hardware and firmware. A native iPhone app may not even run on an older revision or model of iPhone, again, because the OS, hardware or firmware may not be supported. With a native app, the app is downloaded and stored permanently on the device, meaning that it's available for use at all times – even if there is no Internet connectivity.

Web apps are different. A web app is not downloaded or stored on the device, meaning that without an Internet connection, it is not possible to run the app. Web apps are essentially websites which have been designed to mimic, or emulate, a native app in look and feel. As the web app is really a website, whenever you want to run the web app, you access it via the web browser on the device. An advantage of this approach is that most smartphones or tablets can access the web app, regardless of the OS, hardware, or firmware being used on the particular device.

Another advantage of the web app model is that the web app can be updated and tweaked as regularly as you like without requiring the user to download an updated app to their device. This is because all code is stored server-side on the website itself.

Web apps are normally written (or 'coded') in a language that is interpreted by the web browser at run time. The most obvious and popular of these languages is the Internet stalwart HTML. Javascript is also used heavily in web apps to provide some of the more advanced functionalities including menus, transition effects, etc.

Web apps and HTML5
HTML/Javascript can provide a passable user experience for a web app but, as neither of these technologies is new, they have never been able to provide the rich and immersive user experience that native apps could. That's changing quite rapidly though with the introduction of the latest revision of the HTML standard called HTML5.

HTML5 takes things to a whole new level, offering features and Application Programming Interfaces (APIs) that allow websites built on HTML5 to be far more interactive, immersive, visually impressive and, ultimately, more user-friendly than websites built with HTML 4.x. This means that web apps built on HTML5 (running on a device that has a browser capable of correctly interpreting HTML5 pages) can really rival a native app running on the same system.

Features such as geolocation (where the web app can query the device to find out its physical location), orientation detection (where the web app can determine which orientation the device is being held in and redraw the page to suit), local storage (forget cookies – HTML5 supports local SQL databases), enhanced graphics support, etc. all serve to show how much more mobile-friendly the HTML standard is becoming.

Obviously, there is still one major disadvantage with web apps: *no Internet connection, no web app*. This is a biggie; If your device supports 3 or 4G, then chances are you can get online pretty much anywhere, however if your device only has wi-fi, then you won't be able to get to your favourite web app if you aren't near a wi-fi network.

Let's go Native
Even though I love web apps, for the purposes of this book they take a back seat while we focus on the things that you need to do in order to develop and market your native app. Having said that, web apps are a fantastic way to get an understanding of how a native app should look and feel, and I encourage you to throw something together if you have prior HTML knowledge. It's easier to write a web app than a native app, and doing so will give you some good insights into how your native app should be written.

Before I started on my Top-Tens iPhone app, I developed a web app called iViewr. I took all of the location-based data that I had put together for my now defunct website (called expodition.com) and exposed it all on iViewr.com in a web app-friendly way. The exercise was useful for me as it gave me an appreciation of working with such a small screen and viewport. I was able to easily modify UI features and see the results on my iPhone in seconds. If you're new to programming, building a web app might be a good first step towards eventually building and shipping a fully fledged native app. I certainly found it a useful exercise.

The Bottom Line:
Web apps are cool, but native apps are where the money is. And you want to make money, right? Also, you can't really charge for a web app. Well, you *might* be able to charge for the content accessed through the web app, but in reality you won't make much money from this model; far better to write a native app and sell it. You'll find this approach much more financially rewarding.

LESSON 2: THIS IS GOING TO BE SO EASY!

"Writing an iPhone app is going to be so easy! I mean, it's only a smartphone, right? Why worry about research and testing the app with end-users? I can probably crank this little puppy out over a weekend or two and get it up on an App store in next to no time. Then, just wait for the money to come rolling in!"

That's not the way to think about developing your app. I'll explain why: A lot of budding app developers are under the misconception that, because the app they want to produce is a smartphone app running on a handheld or tablet device, writing it will be much less of an undertaking than writing a 'proper' application for a Mac or Windows computer. After all, it's only a mini app for a mini device, so it can't be that difficult, right? Wrong.

It's important to understand that writing an app for a smartphone or tablet device, with their advanced, multi-touch Operating Systems, location awareness, and innovative sensors that can tell proximity and orientation, can be just as difficult and time consuming as writing an app for a desktop system – especially when you also take into account the unique security and privacy concerns that apply to devices which many users take with them wherever they go; just because it's 'scaled down', doesn't mean that it'll be easy to develop.

Don't expect your app to become a hit.
The second thing you need to understand is that you will not become rich overnight. Repeat after me "I will not become rich overnight. I will *not* become rich overnight".

Of course, *someone* will become rich overnight by writing a smartphone app and putting it up for sale. But, sadly, it's unlikely that that person will be you. Yes, if you're lucky, you'll likely make *some* money from your app. It might even make you rich some day if it's mega- successful. But overnight? No way, no how. I'm not trying to put you off, here – I just want you to set your expectations correctly.

Yes it's *possible* that the app you're developing, or thinking of developing, will turn out to be the best thing since sliced bread. However, your hopes will probably be dashed if you set your expectations too high; remember, you're about to enter an ultra-competitive market where the numbers of failures far outweigh the numbers of successes. So be realistic and set your sights and targets appropriately.

The three Ds
The first question you need to ask yourself is: "Am I capable of Designing, Developing and Delivering a smartphone app?" And when you answer, be honest.
Let's look at each of these three Ds in turn:

Design
For a smartphone app to be successful, an awful lot of thought has to go into the initial design stages. Before even a single line of code has been written, you should have a good handle on your app and its functionalities; how will it look? How will it function? What features will it have? What will it do? What won't it do?

The design phase is critical – get things wrong here and you'll end up wasting a lot of time later as you try to shoehorn in features and functionality that you simply forgot about, or neglected to add, in the design phase.

When you have a clear vision of your app, it's important to get feedback at this early stage from others. Be aware, though, that friends and family will very likely give your app the 'thumbs-up' even if they're not entirely convinced of it's worth or marketability. This is because, as friends and/or family, they want to encourage you on your new venture.

So take what they say with a pinch of salt. Better yet, try to get feedback from people you don't know. Don't worry – it's highly unlikely that they'll pinch your idea, run out and buy a Mac, download the SDK, purchase a couple of iPhone programming books, buy sandals, grow a beard, learn Objective C, and beat you to the punch. But if they do, note that I said it's "highly unlikely", and not that it was "impossible" for them to do so.

This is an important stage. Get this wrong and you'll regret it later.

You'll learn more about these important areas in *Lesson 3: Research? Who needs it?* and *Lesson 4: User Interface Guidelines are for nerds.*

Develop

Once you've got the design stage sewn up, you'll need to start looking at writing code. If you're a developer wanting to create an iPhone app, this will be relatively straightforward. Apple's iPhone SDK is a breeze to use; it's very intuitive and allows you to get up to speed quickly. Similarly, Google, Palm, Microsoft and RIM all produce Software Development Kits that enable you to develop apps for their devices with relative ease. Some are easier to get along with than others, but they all provide a great environment to develop apps in.

In addition, there are hundreds of development resources available on the Internet – from Apple's own developer website and iTunes U, where you can download Sanford University or WWDC (Worldwide Developers Conference) training seminars, to the host of other third-party websites that have sprung up to service the needs of budding developers like you.

If you're new to programming, stop right there and step away from the vehicle! Everyone is different, of course, but don't think it will be easy for a newcomer like you to write a smartphone app, because it isn't. I'd guess that the majority of people who try to develop an app from scratch by following tutorials on websites and reading books give up by the time they get to the chapter on *Designing and Implementing View Controllers.*

If this is your situation, then you might want to hire a developer to do all the heavy lifting for you. While this **approach can** prove to be costly (depending on the complexity of the app and how knowledgeable the developer is) you are more likely to end up with a shipping end product than if you try to go it alone as a newbie.

You'll learn more about this in *Lesson 10: Who needs developers?*

Deliver

As the saying goes "No man is an island". The same applies to your app. It's important to realise that you cannot simply write an app, plonk it on an App store and expect the sales to flow. Your app has to be complemented in many different ways in order to stimulate sales and delight your customers. While it's listing in the Android Marketplace or Apple's App store is a good start, you'll need to augment this in many different ways in order to really deliver your app to the world.

The obvious, and most important, way is with a website. Your app's listing in any App store is limited; you're probably only allowed a small selection of images, you very likely won't be allowed video of your app in action, etc. So why not create a basic website where you can throw all of that stuff together in one place?

While you're at it, add a Frequently Asked Questions page so that potential customers can get answers to the things they've been wondering about. Add some prominent contact links and maybe even a forum where users can discuss all aspects of your app and even get technical support from you and, importantly, others. Get the idea?

All of these things show potential customers that you're serious about your app and your customer's experience with it. This makes them more willing to purchase your app.

Lastly, don't forget video sharing sites. If you do create a video of your app in action, post it up on YouTube, Vimeo and as many other video sharing site as you can – the wider you post, the more people will see it, resulting in more traffic to either your website or the app's page on its App store. And it goes without saying that your video should be innovative, interesting and fun!

You'll learn more about these in Lesson *7: Why worry about the users?* and *Lesson 9: Who needs Social Networks?*

The Roadmap

You might be thinking that you're not a product manager so why would you need a roadmap? After all, you've Designed, Developed, and Delivered and your app is finally on sale! No more late nights. No more debugging! Yahooooo! You might think; I'll never have to debug a line of code again.

Well, if you think that getting your app on sale is the end of the process, you'd better think again. If you're really serious about making some money with your app, you need to plan for the long haul. And that means putting on your product management hat and developing a roadmap.

A roadmap allows you to see the bigger picture. It allows you to plan your development efforts so that your short term goals are extremely clear and well defined, and your long term plans, while being a bit looser, are still in place. A good roadmap allows you to see and manage these short and long term plans with ease.

When developing a roadmap, (and especially thinking long term), learn to think outside the box. If you're too conservative with your long term plans, your product will quickly lose out to the competition; blue-sky thinking is essential in the long term.

To help create your roadmap, you'll need to brainstorm and bounce ideas off of your colleagues, friends or even partners. In my case, I always find my kids are great sounding boards. They sometimes come out with wacky ideas that I used to not bother noting down. But I've come to realise it's important to note *everything* down. Features you'd like to see, things you think are easy to do, things you think are impossible to do, etc. As long as you get a healthy set of ideas, you can soon start distilling them down into more manageable categories. Eventually, you'll be able to see what fits in the short, mid, and long term goal categories.

Your roadmap should also take into account market trends and technology forecasts. For example, if you foresee a new version of your device's OS that will include a new technology, or a new hardware feature that is scheduled to be released, build this into your roadmap so that you'll be well prepared to update your product at the most opportune time.

It's also worth remembering that your roadmap is a living document. It's subject to change as development marches forward and milestones are met. You'll find that you may have to prioritise (or re-prioritise) sections of it – and that's fine; the time you have worry is when your roadmap becomes static and stagnant.

Once your app is available for purchase, it's important to make sure that you keep it updated. This is important for two reasons:

• *It keeps your users happy.* It's a fact of life that your app will contain bugs. All apps do – so why would yours be any different? Updates fix this.

• *It keeps interest up in your app.* There's nothing worse than working 'till you almost drop on an app, and then not bothering to update it after the first release. Interest fades on apps that are seen as dormant. Updates reinvigorate your app and generally are accompanied by a modest sales spike.

If done correctly a roadmap will assist you in planning the future development of your app, thus ensuring interest in your app is maintained over an extended period of time.

Be Inspired

I love the story about two shoe salesmen who make an arduous journey to a remote village in an African country. When they got there, the first salesman wanted to turn right back; he called his boss and said "Get us out of here! These people don't wear or want shoes!" The second salesman, seeing the massive opportunity before him, immediately ordered a shipment of shoes, telling his boss "we've got zero competition here! These shoes are gonna sell like hotcakes!"

When you're researching or developing your app, look around you. Be inspired by your environment and the things you do, both mundane and exciting. Look at things in a different way and, above all, be creative with your thoughts. Apps are funny things; sometimes the most unlikely of apps catches the imaginations of millions. If your app can do this, you may well just have a blockbuster on your hands.

The Bottom Line:
Don't underestimate the hurdles and difficulty you will encounter while attempting to bring your app to market. It takes hard work, resilience and commitment to get your app from that idea in your head to a quality, working, and shipping end product. Being innovative with your thoughts and ideas will help you immensely with the task ahead.

LESSON 3: RESEARCH? WHO NEEDS IT?

"Conducting research costs a lot of money, so why bother? Anyway, I already know who's going to buy my app. I don't need to waste my time asking a bunch of people a bunch of questions that I already know the answers to. As far as I'm concerned, I'm gonna cut to the chase and get coding!"

I'm always guilty of letting this one slide whenever I start a project. Don't make the same mistake. Research is fundamental and key to the success of any project. If it's your intention to write a successful smartphone app, you'll need to commit a lot of time to it – and a good chunk of that time should be devoted to research.

Research will help you to define your app by, for example, 'firming up' ideas that you had been thinking of implementing, but were unsure of. By conducting the right type of research you can take a woolly idea for an app and turn it into a solid requirements document, from which you can base your app development.

Research doesn't have to be expensive! Many developers are put off because they believe research will cost them more money than they can afford. Don't make this mistaken assumption. Yes, if you hire someone to come on board and perform research for you, costs might start mounting up. But why not cut out the middleman and do all the research yourself? That way, you get it for free!

There are two main types of product research that you'll need to look at: pre-ship (i.e. before your app goes on sale) and post-ship (carried out after your app goes on sale). Let's discuss both types:

Pre-ship product research
By starting your research at an early age, you'll get to understand exactly what the customer wants before you even fire up the SDK and start writing your first lines of code.

For instance, you might think it's a great idea for your app to be able to display a specific piece of information in four different ways instead of the more usual two. But for 95% your customers, that's overkill that would lead to a cluttered and less elegant interface.

If done correctly, your research would have told you this – allowing you to scale back on that feature, thus cutting your development time and minimizing the risks of bugs creeping in.

Essentially, pre-ship product research allows you to identify and focus on the features that are important to your potential customers, while discarding the 'noise' that would only serve to slow down and complicate your efforts to get your app to market.

There are many accepted forms of conducting pre-ship research, but essentially the research will consist of these tasks:

- Identifying potential users of your app
- Asking the potential users questions
- Recording their responses
- Analyzing these responses

Identifying users
Identifying potential users who will help you conduct research should be relatively straightforward as *long as you know your target market*. For example, if your app is a social networking client designed to help mothers of newborn babies get in touch and share tips and advice, there's no point in roping your

86 year-old grandmother, or your favourite uncle, in for research is there?

Instead, find out when the local mothers and toddlers group meets up and attend the next meet, clipboard in hand. You'll come away with a wealth of information and, importantly, you'll have started the marketing ball rolling with the mothers who answer your questions.

What questions should I ask?

OK – so you've found some people who are willing to give you 15 minutes of their time to answer some questions. Great! But what are you going to ask them? This very much depends on the type of app that you have in mind and so you should think carefully here; if you don't ask the right questions, your research will be flawed from the very beginning. Find out what the 'pain points' are that your app intends to address. How do the participants currently get around these pain points? Do they use apps already on the market? How much are they willing to spend on an app? Do they even know what an app is? As you attempt to determine questions to ask remember to do the following:

Make a list

It seems obvious, but it's critical that you make a list and stick to it. This helps ensure that you ask your subjects the same set of questions, as this will make analysis of the results much easier later on. As touched on above your list should contain a wide variety of questions, and should also include questions that you believe you already know the answer to. Because you probably don't.

Be assertive

You want to get the best out of your research and, as you'll only have a limited amount of time with the participants, make sure you make the most of this time. If responses are rambling, don't hesitate to bring things back on track; failure to do so could result in a wasted session.

Wisdom in crowds

How you conduct your research will vary depending on your proposed app. In the example above, a local mothers and toddlers group would be ideal if your app was designed for that target market – but such well defined groups are not always that easy to find. In this scenario, you might want to explore other ways of conducting research. For example you might want to perform surveys on the street by stopping people and asking them a set of relevant questions that you record on a clipboard. This form of research can be hit or miss, but there's no denying that there's wisdom in crowds. Choose the correct spot and you'll get great feedback.

Privacy concerns

Be sensitive to the fact that the participants of your research session may not be happy about divulging personal information to you, or in front of other participants. While this information may not seem particularly interesting to you, it may not be the same for the participant. Therefore, it always makes sense ask if the participants may want to give you their responses privately. In addition, you may want to produce a permission form that can be handed to participants, granting you permission to use their responses in the future (for example, in marketing or promotional material).

Recording answers

Asking questions is just one half of the story. Recording answers (and more importantly recording answers accurately) is just as important. Obviously, the method you use to record your answers will vary depending on the method you've employed to ask the questions.

If you are recording a group, video recording is a great way to capture their responses. In this scenario, first ensure that your group are happy to be filmed. Once they agree, get them all in one location and set that camera rolling. In this type of set-up, try to limit participation down to 7 or 8 people.

Hand-held recorders are a fantastic way of capturing feedback from participants and I urge you to, at minimum, use one of these devices. Remember, your smartphone can probably do a great job of recording voice, so you don't even need to buy any additional hardware!

Analyzing your results

The last stage of your pre-ship research is to analyze the results. This task will be made much easier if you ensured that you asked everyone the same set of questions! Look for trends in your participants' responses. Look for strong opinions, but don't overlook the comments from participants who may be slightly backward about coming forward. Essentially, this stage requires painstakingly collating responses (maybe from different sources such as paper forms, video or audio recordings) and putting them in a form that you, and others, can see easily – for example, in a spreadsheet.

The trends you'll see in these responses will indicate to you what features you need to implement in your app and what features you can safely put on the back-burner for v2.0. Some of these features will probably already be in your plans, while others will be new to you. Those are the ones we want to capture.

Post-ship product research
Product research can also be carried out after your app has shipped. This post-ship research can tell you important things about your app such as what you did right, and what you did wrong that needs changing.

Too many developers spend months of effort writing and developing an app, only to forego collecting user feedback about the app once it has been shipped. This is unforgivable if you are serious about your app! For example, there may be UI or design issues that you simply won't know about until you ask your users what their thoughts are on the usability of your app. These are the things that, typically, your users will not bother to tell you about *unless* you ask them – so don't miss the opportunity.

As we'd expect, there may be features that are simply missing (maybe you didn't think it worthwhile adding these features in this version. Or maybe you just didn't think about them!). Either way your users will notice these, so why not give them the opportunity to tell you all about it? This type of feedback can, and should, find its way onto your roadmap for possible inclusion into future versions of your app.

Maybe there's something wrong with the 'flow' of your app. Maybe the non-standard fonts you're using are grating, distracting, or hard to read? Maybe your app just doesn't do what it's supposed to do, or crashes every so often. Post-ship research will tell you all about it.

Research methods
There are varied ways of conducting post-ship research. For example, why not do this from your app's website via a simple questionnaire or survey?

Alternatively, why not create a test script containing steps that the user needs to complete in specific order? Then, manhandle, cajole, persuade or otherwise induce some participants into working through the test script for you. Again, this will give you valuable feedback as to how your app is performing 'in the field', and will also highlight the things you need to focus on when you produce your next update.

In some ways, this 'post-ship' product research provides much more meaningful results than the 'pre-ship' product research, where results can be misleading due to the fact that, effectively, you're talking about vapourware as your product doesn't actually exist yet.

Act on it
Above all, if your users take the time to respond to your questions and provide you with feedback, act on it! Don't leave that valuable feedback sitting in a corner somewhere, only to be forgotten with the march of time. That's just not cricket, is it?.

The Bottom Line:
Careful research, both before and after your app ships, is crucial in order to understand what your potential customers *want* from your product and what your existing customers are actually *getting*. Ignore it at your peril.

LESSON 4: USER INTERFACE GUIDELINES ARE FOR NERDS

"How difficult can it be? There's no science to this, after all. I put a button here, a button there, a drop-down thingy on the left and a slider on the right. Sorted!"

Well... not quite. When designing your interface there are guidelines that you should stick to in order to ensure that your user has the best experience possible while interacting with your app. An app designed with attention to detail and a good set of User Interface guidelines will be a pleasure to use; apps that disregard these guidelines are destined for the scrapheap. And we don't want that to happen to *your* app, do we?

Even though users of your app might not have a degree in User Interface (UI) design, they can still instinctively tell when something doesn't work in the way that it probably should do.

In most cases of bad UI design, it's plainly obvious to the user that the designer of the app has put little thought into the way in which the app will be used. In some cases, this realisation might only be on a subconscious level. But trust me, conscious or subconscious, they'll be able to tell. And the kicker is, when your app doesn't 'feel' right to someone, they'll be less inclined to return to it in the future. After all, people like using things that surprise and delight them, and not things that turn them off. Not surprisingly, these users won't then recommend your app to others. As you'll see in upcoming lessons, recommendations are one of the engines that can really get your sales going, but they'll only come from users who have had positive experiences with your app.

So your mission, should you choose to accept it, is to create a UI that will delight users of your app, and entice them to use it again and again. Sound simple? Well, in reality, it is.

As long as you stick to the guidelines.

Looking good!

Your app has to look good. There are no two ways about it. Nobody likes using an app that looks like it was designed with a fork; it's just not on. So really think about the way that your users will use your app and design the interface accordingly.

While designing Top-Tens, I knew I wanted the user to see the content as soon as the app opened, much like the iPhone's *Weather* app. With that app, you open it, and it shows you the weather. There are no menus to navigate and no additional windows to open, and why should there be? Want to see the weather in another town or region? Simply swipe left or right.

I wanted to replicate this simplicity with Top-Tens. Essentially, I looked at the UI of a well- designed app and decided that I didn't want to re-invent the wheel – if users are comfortable with existing paradigms that work well, why not emulate them in your app? It's important to note that I'm not advocating ripping off another app's UI here, but rather just pointing out that using paradigms that work well is something that's worth doing. I did just that, and loosely based the Top-Tens UI on the Weather app's UI, and found that it worked really well. Important: If you do base your UI on an existing app, remember to be respectful of that other developer's hard work. In other words, don't rip it off.

So when you open Top-Tens, you see a list populated with the current top 10 books, for example, from Amazon. If you want to see what the top 10 songs on iTunes are, you swipe left. Simple.

Of course, I made some mistakes. For example, my app doesn't have the gorgeous artwork that accompanies each page on the Weather app. I would have loved it if it did, but I didn't have the time or the funds to get that sorted, and so I ended up doing all of the artwork for the app myself. Don't get me wrong, I'm a dab-hand at Photoshop, but I'm no expert. So other than the basic interface elements (like the numbers denoting each top 10) I left the app pretty much graphics-free.

In a way, users have been spoiled with some of the fantastic visual treats that app developers have delivered recently – Apple's very own GarageBand for iPad is an excellent case in point; it's simply stunning to look at with it's highly detail and thoroughly realistic instruments, it has to be the most impressive (non-game) app I've had the pleasure of using on an iOS device. As Steve Jobs would say "it's gorgeous".

Users really notice the quality of the artwork in an app, and so this is an area that I thoroughly recommend you invest in. When your app is finally on sale, you really won't regret the money you spent on getting some cool artwork done.

While you can't really go too far with lovely graphics, there are times when you do need to put the reins on. For example, subtle animations serve to add another dimension to your UI and are definitely the way to go. When a button is tapped, it's nice to see some indication that the tap 'event' was recognised by the app, maybe by the button glowing momentarily, or even increasing in size subtly before decreasing back to its normal size. These touches give the user feedback that they pressed the right button. And they look cool, too.

But remember, be subtle. While that animation might look cool the first few times you see it, it can start to become quite jarring and even annoying the more you see it. Subtle animations are barely noticeable; anything else can become a distraction. In a worst case scenario they can interfere with the flow of work, generally get in the way, and even slow things down. If they do that, even for a microsecond, they need to go!

Iconic interaction

Take a look at the home screen of your smartphone or tablet. See how the calendar icon is instantly recognizable? And the email icon, too? Why do you think they're like this? The answer is that the people who created those icons put an awful lot of time, thought and effort into making them highly effective, static visual representations of the apps they will launch when tapped. While it may sound like a lofty goal, this should also be your aim with the icon for your app.

Your app's icon is the first thing the user sees when they start interacting with your app. An attractive, well designed icon will draw the user in to your app; It will scream at them "press me, press me!" And if yours doesn't, you're putting your app at an instant disadvantage.

Your icon must look professional and attractive – anything else and you're in trouble. When creating your icon, start with a 512x512 pixel workspace so that when it's scaled down it'll still look crisp. I've seen fellow developers submit smaller icons for their apps and when they're resized in iTunes, for example, they look rubbish. Make sure you avoid that.

The key is not to leave your icon design until the last minute. You won't be able to spend as much time as you want on it, so start it early in the process. For example, the research phase is a great time to start sketching out ideas for an icon. Why not show these icon idea sketches to your research participants and ask them what they believe the icon signifies? If you're lucky, you'll be able to discount some ideas really early on and focus on the ones that make much more sense.

Oh, and generally the simpler an icon is, the better. It's that simple!

Be consistent

When designing your UI, ensure that you treat your interface elements and controls in a consistent manner. For example, if the user performs a particular gesture to initiate an action in one area of your app, ensure that they can use that same gesture to perform similar actions in other areas of the app. Similarly make sure that if you use the same icon in different parts of the app, that icon always performs the same action. Failure to adhere to these basic points will mean that you end up with confounded and frustrated users because the app they're using does things inconsistently.

It always irks me when I read something somewhere and I see the same term being used in the same location or publication inconsistently. For example, I read a document on MySQL recently that freely interchanged two other variants of its spelling (mySQL and MySql) throughout the document. It grated on me every time I saw it and actually detracted from what I was reading as my focus turned from the content of the document, to how many more times I could spot the inconsistency!

So be consistent in all areas of your app. For example, if your app labels a button or view MySQL, ensure that every other use of the term MySQL in your app follows the same convention and spelling. Ideally, your UI should melt into the background. Don't give your UI the opportunity to distract your user and detract from the important thing in your app: it's content.

Don't be Picky

As well as consistency inside your app, don't forget to be consistent outside of it. For example, depending on the device and platform you're writing your app for, your development environment, or SDK, will most likely provide you with standard icons and controls to include in your projects. Make sure to use them. If there are system-provided Date Pickers, then use them. If the system provides Pickers for lists or other types of content, then save yourself time and effort and use those too.

It's just not worth trying to recreate the wheel. And for another thing, it's unlikely that you'll do any better than the standard objects that you've been provided with. Further, as these elements will be used in other apps and the system itself, users of your app will be familiar with them and their usage. They also serve to give your app 'polish'. And you want to give your app polish, don't you?

It makes sense to study other apps, just as I did, to determine the things that they do well and the things they don't do as well. For example, if you plan on using lists in your app, look at how lists are handled in a few other apps. Are you able to identify any good or bad points? Do those apps allow the user to sort and edit lists easily? Will yours?

Diff'rent strokes

Your app should always provide your user with the standard and expected interaction methods that are used both in the Operating System and in other apps. Nowadays, most smartphones and tablets use touch screens which pave the way for the usage of gestures and strokes as an input method. In a relatively short space of time, users have now become familiar, and comfortable, with this mode of operation. Therefore, your app should provide for this and fully support the strokes and gestures that are available and provided through your development kit. Failing to provide support for gestures will inevitably result in many "What'chu talkin' about..." moments when your app fails to respond or work as expected.

Device differences

When designing the UI for your app, remember to take into account the device that the app will be used on. There will be subtle differences in the way an app is used on a smartphone when compared to the way the same app is used on a tablet. Don't take the easy option and simply scale up your smartphone app's UI for a tablet-sized interface; bigger isn't always better as the saying goes. Similarly, don't add features to your tablet app with reckless abandon simply because you have more screen real estate to fill.

Be smart about your choices and find new and interesting ways to present your content on a bigger screen. For example, on a Smartphone, you won't be able to get away from displaying (and switching between) several different screens of information depending on what information you want to provide your users. However on a tablet with a properly designed UI taking advantage of the larger screen area, you'll likely be able to display all information on the same screen (using split screen views, etc.) thus minimising, or even eliminating, any transitions.

Don't leave it to the device!
Let's use the iPhone/iPad as an example, here. If you're going to the trouble of writing an iPhone app, take the extra time to tailor it so that it works on the other devices, too – and don't just leave it to the system to do all the heavy lifting for you.

Yes, an iPhone app will work on an iPad without any tweaking due to the iPad's ability to 'pixel- double' an app. However, the results are less than stellar. In this mode, the app simply runs in the middle of the iPad screen with every pixel doubled, effectively doubling the size of the running app. Look, the iPad gives you a gorgeous 9.7inch screen – so use every last pixel with care and attention! When an app is pixel-doubled, it takes up the entire screen but at what appears to be a low resolution – so you see all the jagged edges of text and some images.

Far better to write your app so that it determines what device it's running on, and then shows the user the best interface for that device. This way, running your app on an iPhone will result in a UI that fits nicely on the iPhone (or iPod touch) screen, whereas running your app on an iPad enables the UI to re-jig itself and utilise the entire iPad screen.

Sensors
Most smartphones or tablets on the market nowadays incorporate a host of different sensors that allow the device to determine a wide variety of things about its state and location. Proximity sensors tell the device if it's near to something (for example, an ear) allowing the device to then turn the screen off. Ambient light sensors tell the device if the room is dark, allowing the screen brightness to automatically be reduced to avoid burning the user's retinas. Orientation sensors tell the device which way up it is, and the list goes on.

Ensure that you make use of these sensors in your app *if it makes sense to do so*. Nowadays, people expect an app to change its orientation when the device's orientation changes. So if it makes sense for your app to do this, then implement it. Of course, this might not always apply to every app – for example, Angry Birds would look kinda dumb in portrait mode, don't you think?

Keep the User Informed

It's frustrating when you're trying to do something but you can't tell if the app has finished what its doing or is still working away in the background. So always implement things like Activity Indicators that keep the user informed about the task in hand. Activity Indicators don't have to tell the user when the activity is expected to end, they simply show that something is happening. If you are doing any type of activity that you believe may take some time, then keep the user informed.

With other types of alerts and notifications, make these short and to the point, but never cryptic. You will probably be working with a small screen space and so you need to word your alerts and messages very carefully so that they don't end up confusing your users. Also, take into account the orientation of the device when deciding on the wording – a message may look great in Landscape orientation, but might appear truncated or mis-aligned when the device is rotated to Portrait.

Obey the rules

The topics discussed in this chapter only touch the surface, and serve to get you thinking about this important piece of the app-creation puzzle. Good UI design is universal in that the concepts, rules and ideas that apply for an iPhone, for instance, can be applied successfully to other types of smartphone. As with most things there may be exceptions, though, and so I would advise you to review the UI guidelines for your device and adhere to those.

The Bottom Line:

In many ways, your User Interface is where your product will either shine or crash and burn. Don't assume that throwing a few system-provided interface elements onto a blank canvas will do the job just because they are system provided. You need to think carefully about how your app will be used, and design the interface accordingly. Lastly, make your app a joy to use, and not a chore.

LESSON 5: TO-DO OR NOT TO-DO?

"Sure... my app has to be a little different from what's already on the market, but it doesn't have to be groundbreaking! Just having a working app on sale will be enough for me. I'm sure people don't want an app with all the bells and whistles, anyway – as long as it does the job without crashing, they'll be happy. Anyhow, I'm not the most creative of people – I'll leave all the flashy stuff to the others!"

Ok – I get it. So your To-Do list is brown, when the majority of the others in the App store are white. And your To-Do list gives you the ability to sort your To-Dos alphabetically and chronologically. At the same time, too! Fantastic!

But at the end of the day, it's still a To-Do list. And the app store is littered with them. This tells me a few things:

•   People lack imagination. There are already a million other To-Do list apps on sale so why put up yet another one? OK – so you wrote it just to get an understanding of how to write an iPhone app. Well... why didn't you learn how to create an app with something a little more... exciting? Marketable? Unique? Maybe something you could actually sell on the store and make some money from? But no, you went with a brown To-Do list that sorts your To-Dos alphabetically and chronologically. Great.

• There *is* a market in To-Do lists. There sure is. And it's good to get involved in a 'hot' market segment. But if you are going to be involved in that new segment, make sure that what you're developing wipes the floor with the competition. Make your offering stand out from the crowd by decking it out with truly innovative and differentiating features. After all, if you don't have anything new to bring to the table, then why bother?

• If you are thinking of writing a To-Do list app to sell on an App store, think again. When I set out to create Top-Tens, I knew I wanted to do something different – something that wasn't already available in the App store, but initially, I wasn't sure exactly what that would be.

I thought about how people use a smartphone, how they hold it, and what they use it for. I looked at my own smartphone usage and realised that 90% of the time, I used my iPhone for short periods of time. I'd turn it on, open an app (like email, weather, or stocks, etc.) check for the latest, then close the app down.

This usage pattern made me think that I'd want to create an app that works in a similar way; something the user could open, get the latest information about something, and then close down again when they were done. That's when the idea of constantly updating top 10 lists came to me - and the ideas behind my app started to take shape.

Think outside the box
For some people, creative thinking comes easy. If you are accustomed to 'thinking outside the box' then chances are you can come up with a worthwhile idea for a smartphone app. If thinking outside the box is not your thing, then you've got a difficult task ahead of you.

With over 350,000 apps in Apple's App store, over 200,000 in the Android Marketplace, 10,000 in the Windows Marketplace, etc. yours has got to be something special to stand out. Don't just write 'another (insert your own generic app type here) app'; that won't get you many column inches. To coin that old Apple marketing term, *Think different*. Think unique, but also think obvious. Many of the successful apps in the app store are pretty simple in nature, not too complex and are the type of thing that gets people saying "I wish I'd thought of that!"

31

Well here's your chance. The more thought you put into your app in these early stages, the more chance there is of you producing something worthwhile and something that's capable of generating buzz in the media as well as interest in your potential customer base, which will hopefully translate into a successful launch of your app.

Make me laugh

Looking at the types of apps which go viral extremely quickly, it's obvious that apps that make people laugh are constantly at the top of the charts. Everyone loves a laugh and so if you're not quite sure of the app you want to write or the direction you want to go down, give some serious thought into this area. But remember - farting apps are so passé now, darling. So don't even go there.

Apps that make people laugh are more likely to spread virally by Social networks and services such as Twitter and Facebook, driven by the feel good factor they provide. If you believe you have what it takes then what are you waiting for?

Problem Solver

Look at the things you've done in the last 24 hours. Man, you did a lot of things! But could any of them have been done a little easier? Could your shopping trip have been less stressful with a tailored app that helped you with your purchases? What about your visit to the gym? Or the hour spent in front of TV watching your favourite show? Or the dead time spent riding the bus?

The majority of us go through our daily lives doing things that we've done time and time again. Some of these are fun, some are chores and some are problematic, however our ability to adapt has enabled us to overcome these problems to the extent that we actually no longer see them as problems. Instead, they just become a series of steps that we've carried out many times before and will probably carry out many times again in the future. You know what? There's an app for that. And if you don't create it, someone else will.

Smart by name

Smartphones nowadays are not only smart by name; they're really smart by nature. Of course, the same applies to tablets, too. With their ability to detect your location, access the internet and even know which direction they're facing, some pretty cool applications can be written which take advantage of these capabilities. Make sure to exploit them when you're designing your app.

What about the competition?

Remember, as you read this, there are hundreds of thousands of developers actively working on mobile apps. The chances are, some of them will be working on an app similar to the one you plan on writing. It's also very likely that many of these apps have already shipped – so the app store will probably already contain numerous apps that perform the same functions as your intended app. Collectively these apps are known as: *The Competition.*

Know your enemy

It goes without saying that for your app to become a success, it has to sell more than the competition. But how can you ensure that this will be the case? Well, you need to have a good handle on the competition in the first place. Your app will be competing with these apps for sales. You'll be chasing the same customer and competing for the same column inches, both online and in print. All of this means that you'll need to get to know the competition. Intimately.

Buy before you try

Isn't it great to have a try before you buy option when venturing into the unknown? Be it an iPhone app that you're unsure of splashing out .99p for, or a demo version of a software program for your Windows PC or Mac costing several hundred dollars. Try before you buy can help you sort the wheat from the chaff by allowing you to take an app through its paces before you decide on buying it.

But when you're a developer putting together a smartphone app, you'll need to reverse that sentiment by *buying* first before trying to develop. You see, by buying 4 or 5 apps which are similar to the one you plan on creating, you can get a good handle on what works and what doesn't. It also makes sense to buy the full version of the app as opposed to the free version – the free version will be lacking functionality that you'd probably want to see.

Remember *Lesson 3: Research? who needs it?* Well, the chances are that at least half of the developers of those 4 or 5 apps that you have just purchased have conducted research of their own. So it makes sense to see what, if anything, they learned and how they went about implementing things.

Benchmark testing is always good to do. If the apps you're testing against all perform similar functions (such as connecting to the Internet to download lists of data) then make sure your app is competitive. For example, my Top-Tens app connects to my servers over the Internet to download regularly updated information. I compared the response times for my app with apps that did similar things – RSS Reader apps, the Weather app, etc. and ensured that my app provided a similar user experience.

Other platforms

When evaluating the competition, don't just stick to your platform of choice. Just because you'll be writing your app for Apple's iOS platform, it doesn't mean that you should ignore Google's Android, or Microsoft's Windows Phone 7 platforms. On the contrary, it's sometimes refreshing to see how similar issues are tackled on other platforms. As strange as it seems, it's probably even a good idea to look at 'proper' Mac and Windows applications, too. You'll be surprised at what you find and the insight they bring.

Turning the tables

If you do things well at some point, the tables will be turned and other developers will be buying *your* app to determine how to implement a particular feature, see how best to organize a UI, or work out the best method of presenting a specific type of data. Of course, you won't know that this is happening, but if you've been creative in your app development and have a good amount of purchases per week, then you can be pretty sure that the competition are scrutinising your work. So give them something worthwhile to look at!

The Bottom Line:

As you're putting together your app, take inspiration from your surroundings and activities to identify gaps that need filling. Look at what others are doing and determine if, and how, you can do better. Don't enter saturated markets unless you can truly bring something unique to the table. Lastly, disregard the competition at your peril.

LESSON 6: AN ELEVATOR PITCH? REALLY!?

"Look – I'm not trying to get a start-up funded, alright? I'm not looking for seed capital, a financial backer, or any of that malarkey. So one thing I really don't need is an elevator pitch. If I want to tell people about my app, I'll just tell them! It's really not that difficult."

Well, without proper preparation, you'll be surprised how difficult it actually is. You see, it's really important to be able to pitch your app to potential buyers succinctly and in such a way that they immediately 'get' it. An elevator pitch (also known as a two-minute pitch) is an ideal way to do this. Its premise is simple: get your app idea across to another party in two minutes or less.

Elevator pitches are not supposed to be a vehicle for you to attempt to impart the minutiae of every nook and cranny of your app onto an unsuspecting audience – that's what app review websites are for. Rather, the elevator pitch should be seen as a way of creating a hook that gets the user interested enough to want to find out more about your app. Which is when they'll be more inclined to read the review on the app review website.

Of course an elevator pitch can, and should, be used anywhere; see that guy in front of you in the grocery store line? He has an Android phone in his hand! I bet he's just dying to hear your two-minute pitch. It's a technique I use a lot. Whenever I see anyone with a smartphone and there's a potential for a quick chat, I'm in there.

I'm surprised by the amount of people who buy my app on the spot after doing a quick search on the App store! I haven't worked out yet if that's because they're just trying to be polite, are maybe intimidated by me (well – I am a 6' 2" gentleman with a bald head and a build to match) or if they generally find my app awesome. But it definitely works, so ensure that the elevator pitch is part of your arsenal.

Creating your pitch
So what does your elevator pitch need to contain? And what do you need to keep *out* of your pitch? Read on to find out:

Keep it brief
Remember, you only have limited time – so this is one of those times where less really is more. Some people are naturally very good at getting their point across and, if you're one of these, then your elevator pitch will be a breeze. For others (like me) you'll need to plan so that you can fit all the things that you want to say into such a short timeframe.

What problem does your app attempt to solve?
This is your hook. What does your app actually do? You've been working on your app for a long time and so you know what it actually does inside out. But articulating that information in as few words as possible is not as easy as it sounds. The very first words you say, that first sentence, can make or break your pitch – so think about this carefully.

I would always end up rambling on about the finer points of my app, finding myself talking for longer and longer about things that weren't that important to the person I was pitching to. In the end, I asked a friend who knew what my app did to pitch it to me. What a revelation! Because he wasn't bogged down with the intricacies of how the app worked, he was able to pitch the main points to me more succinctly than I did to him! If you're having trouble getting your elevator pitch together, it's definitely worth using this trick.

Don't use jargon
OK – so we all know what SaaS and cloud computing is, (shame on you if you don't because that's what Google is for), but does that 14 year old kid

that you're pitching to know? What about the investment banker in her thirties – does she know? These both happen to be potential purchasers of your app, but chances are you'll immediately lose their interest when you mention such things.

My app relies on a MySQL database and multiple PHP scripts running on my web server in order to function correctly. I was proud of the fact that I had created and configured the back- end in that way - and so I found that these facts would manage to slip into any elevator pitches that I was giving. While it made me feel good, it was probably a major turn off to whomever I was pitching to, (not to mention a waste of precious time). They simply did not need to know this – so why tell them? What's that saying? Oh yes – KISS: Keep It Simple, Stupid.

What makes your app different to the others?
In other words, what's the value proposition? Why should the person listening to your pitch buy your app over the others that may already be on sale? In two minutes, it's easy to get caught up in the detail - resulting in you missing the opportunity to highlight the USP (Unique Selling Point) of your app. Make sure that you understand your value proposition and ensure that you communicate it effectively; Give the listener a reason to buy your app!

Don't ask too many questions
One way to derail your pitch is if you pepper it with questions. This gives the person you are pitching to free reign to take you down roads that you didn't intend on going. And if you only have two minutes to get your point across, then you may as well give up now.

Don't get me wrong, it's OK to ask a question or two – especially if you're confident the responses will aid in the delivery of your pitch, but in general ensure that you keep questions to a minimum. Another trick to use when asking questions is to only ask 'closed questions'. Closed questions can normally only be answered with a 'yes' or 'no'. For example, "Do you use your iPhone to book movie tickets?". Depending on the 'yes' or 'no' answer, you can quickly move on to explain how your app improves this process.

Practice makes perfect...
Getting your elevator pitch to flow will require a considerable amount of

practice. It's a performance, after all - and for any performance to wow its audience, the performer needs to invest time rehearsing over and over again until the performance becomes second nature.

The same applies to your elevator pitch. Investing time rehearsing up-front will pay dividends later on when you start converting your pitches to sales.

Initially, practice in front of a mirror until you are confident you have the content and timings right. Why not use your smartphone to video yourself delivering the pitch? By watching and reviewing your performance, you'll be able to fine tune it and work out what works and what doesn't.

Friends, Family and Strangers

When you're happy with the content of your elevator pitch, take the next step of practicing it on friends and family. When you do, make sure they give you honest feedback – since after you've finalized your pitch on them, you'll then move on to delivering this pitch to complete strangers. And complete strangers won't be as nice as friends and family. This is a conundrum that you'll always run into with friends and family, whether you're doing research, practicing elevator pitches or designing icons. They never want to hurt your feelings and so they'll end up telling you what they believe you want to hear even though they know deep down that that elevator pitch you just delivered was as boring and as lacklustre as they come.

Written elevator pitches

This is a much easier proposition – essentially you'll take your existing elevator pitch and put it into writing. You can then send this pitch to prospective interested parties via email. I've used this technique extensively to help market Top-Tens and have been really happy with the results. I've even been able to build up a list of 'friendly' contacts that've read the pitch and decided to post details on their websites or even tweet about it on Twitter. However, there are a few additional things you should be aware of:

Don't spam

Nobody likes Spam (well, apart from the spammers, that is). Average users like you and I hate the stuff, and so be mindful of whom you send your email elevator pitch to. You want your pitch to press the right buttons of the recipient, not get them reacting negatively and chucking your pitch into the junk mail folder. If you're mailing to a large audience, or people you haven't mailed before, always include an 'opt-out' message at the bottom of your email. And if someone does opt out of receiving future email messages from you, remember to action it *immediately* and remove them from your list. If you forget and you mail them again in the future, they won't be too pleased and you could find your email address ending up on a blacklist somewhere which won't do your future marketing efforts any good.

Again, keep it brief

An email elevator pitch should be no more that 100-125 words. Any more than that and it needs a serious re-write. Also, when writing your pitch, break it up into easily digestible sentences and paragraphs

Grammar

One of my pet peeves is a badly written email. In this day and age, there is no excuse for badly written copy containing spelling mistakes or other grammar and punctuation errors. It says one thing about you: You just couldn't be bothered. And if you can't even be bothered to get a 125-word pitch written correctly, what does that say about the quality of your app?

The Bottom Line:

By neglecting to create an elevator pitch, or underestimating its importance, you will not be able to concisely, effectively and successfully convey the features and benefits of your app to potential users.

LESSON 7: WHY WORRY ABOUT THE USERS?

"There's no point in trying to get feedback from users. You only hear the complaints or negative stuff anyway; people only get in touch when they have a problem or when something isn't working. And anyway, I don't have the time to start analyzing email or looking at feedback forms – I'm working on an update to my app!"

Getting feedback from your users is an extremely valuable, and rewarding, exercise. Feedback enables you to see what you've done right with your app and, probably more importantly, what you've done wrong. Feedback enables you to improve your app (maybe by fine tuning or adjusting back-end configurations in a client-server app, or by identifying a bug and coding a fix that can be rolled out in an update) and also provides you with ideas for future versions of your app. If used correctly, feedback allows you to engage, and interact with, your users, giving them the 'feel-good factor' while giving you valuable data to work with.

Make it easy

If you really want to hear from your users, it's really important to make it easy for them to get in touch. For instance, if you've created a website to support your app, assume that visitors to the site will want to contact you via the site - so don't give them the run-around; make sure you have a *Contact Us* link displayed prominently on your home page (and consider displaying it on other pages, too). One of my pet hates is trying to work out how to contact someone after visiting his or her site. I mean... you've gone to all the trouble of creating a product, creating a website, keeping it updated, but you don't want to be contacted about it? Really?!

The same applies to your app. As I've said, feedback is important, and if the user can give that feedback immediately after coming across an issue or problem, the better they will feel. Remember, it's all about the feel-good factor. With Top-Tens, I did it right from inside the app. I made it obvious to the user, as I wanted them to be able to contact me easily.

In the main Top-Tens User Interface, I have five icons. Out of these five navigation and control buttons available to the user, two of them enable the user to contact me!

The *Report* button allows the user to report a problem with any of the top 10 lists that they are attempting to view. Because these lists are updated automatically every 30 minutes, there's a potential that something might go awry in the process and, while I might miss it, the chances are that at least one user of Top-Tens won't. With this button, they can quickly and easily inform me about the problem so I can go about rectifying the issue.

The *Suggest* button allows the user to suggest a new top 10 list that they would like to track. By default, Top-Tens tracks around 100 top 10 lists. However, if I had enough users request (via the Suggest button) that I track say, the top 10 books on the Italian Amazon website, I could easily plug that into the system, allowing every Top-Tens user the option of tracking this list too.

My app is specific to the iOS platform so both the Report and Suggest buttons open the Mail app, (that is present on all iPhones, iPods or iPads), with a pre-formatted and addressed email. This means that all the user has to do is add their specific report or request and click *Send*.

This integration with the 'native' iOS apps makes things easy for you as a developer, while making your app appear more polished to the user. But, more importantly, these buttons allow interaction with me, the developer, in a convenient, easy and intuitive way.

As well as making it easy to contact me, I wanted to make it easy for users of Top-Tens to spread the news about the app with a *Tell a Friend* button. When clicked, this gives the user the option to open the email app and send a message to a friend about Top-Tens.

Acknowledge, and then Act

When you eventually do get feedback from users – be that through email, via your app, or from a feedback form, the two most important things to do are to acknowledge that feedback, and act on it. Why go to all the trouble of making it easy for your users to contact you, if you're not going to bother doing anything with that feedback when they send it?

The chances are that you won't be flooded with emails messages, at least not at the beginning anyway, so attempt to acknowledge each and every email you get from a user. They did spend money on your app, after all. As I was getting a steady stream of messages (especially requests) I decided to make a template that the majority of my email responses could be based on. It was then simple for me to cut and paste the text into an email as necessary and reply to the user. This streamlining allowed me to respond to users rapidly, ensuring that they felt 'listened to' and that their communication didn't just go into a big, black hole.

Technical Support

All software contains bugs. No matter how well you've programmed your app, it will contain bugs. Some will be minor, some will be obscure, some will be humdingers. Some bugs may even originate in the Operating System, or other apps, and only be exposed by your app. Either way, trust me, they'll be there. It also goes without saying that your users will come across these bugs as they use your app. So you need to have something in place to help those users when that occurs.

The good thing is that the majority of users who experience bugs with your app will, for the most part, experience the *same* bugs - this makes it easier to provide assistance.

Let the user 'self-help'

A major objective of providing a successful technical support experience involves enabling the user to 'self-help'. If the user can help themselves to resolve an issue without taking your time, then you're onto a winner - especially if you have many users finding the same bug in your app.

Imagine how much time you'll waste trying to respond to ten emails per day each reporting the same bug? Imagine how much time you'll save if you have a fully documented solution or workaround to the problem on your website? This way your users can find the solution for themselves while browsing your site, or you can send them a link to the solution in an email response to their query.

A fully-fledged Knowledgebase is probably overkill for the types of queries that you'll be encountering. Sure, if you have more than five apps on sale then a Knowledgebase, which allows users to search for known issues and provide them with solutions, will be invaluable. However, if you only have one app on sale, the costs involved in purchasing, setting up and maintaining a proper

Knowledgebase will be prohibitive. In these instances, a FAQ (Frequently Asked Questions) might suffice. Alternatively, a more structured set of pages might be your best option. Whichever option you decide to go with will depend on many things including the complexity of your app, your app's target audience, and more.

It's not just about bugs

Remember though, that technical support isn't just about bugs – sometimes your user just needs to be guided through specific procedures that may not be intuitive or immediately obvious. And remember, if a user can't get an app up and running within a few minutes of installing and starting that app, it's going to get deleted, badly rated, and potentially badly reviewed too.

For example, if your app is a social networking client, it's likely that your user will need to enable an option on their social networking account in order for your app to gain access to their contact information, friend lists, etc. If you believe your app has any of these 'gotcha' scenarios then document them fully, including plain and easy-to-follow steps so that your users can get up and running with the minimum of fuss. After you've gone to all the trouble of documenting these scenarios, don't hide them away! Ensure that they are placed on your app's website in the 'Technical Support' area where they can be easily found. Your users will thank you and, hopefully, you'll thank me for giving you this tip!

The Bottom Line:

By placing feedback and customer interaction low in your list of priorities, you will struggle to identify problems with your app 'in the field'. You'll also find it impossible to determine what users like, and dislike, about your app.

LESSON 8: MARKETING, SCHMARKETING...

"Why in the world would I need a marketing campaign? I'm only a 'one-man-band', not a company or big corporation. Plus, I'm only selling a smartphone app! From what I've heard, these things market themselves, don't they? I'll let some other sucker waste his money on marketing!"

Lots of people think that they can write a killer app, post it up on the App store, and then just sit back and wait for the money to come rolling in. Let's get this straight right away. This will not happen to you. No matter how good your app is, it's not going anywhere without a clever and sustained marketing effort.

I found this out to my cost with Top-Tens. While in the development stages, marketing was the last thing on my mind. I knew I'd have to do some form of marketing when the app went live in the App store, but I honestly thought it would be a trivial task. Naively, I thought my app would capture the imaginations of thousands of iPhone users, who would then recommend it to thousands of others, ad infinitum.

Unfortunately, this didn't happen. And the chances are that you will end up in the same boat. So what can you do to maximize sales of your app?

Develop a marketing strategy

It's obvious really. You need a marketing strategy in order to get people interested in what you're offering. But where do you start? Ideally, your strategy should be focused around the USPs (Unique Selling Points) of your app and how they meet your potential customer's needs and expectations. As these needs and expectations may be constantly changing, your strategy will need to be flexible and easy to change, too.

For most app developers, marketing=getting a few mentions on the app review sites. In reality, it's much more than this. But review sites are as good a place to start as any...

Review Sites

There are countless app review sites on the Internet that can give your app some great exposure. The trick is getting the sites to carry out a review in the first place. You need to get them interested enough in your app for them to set aside time to take your app through its paces and then write about it. Firstly, don't expect any review sites to buy your app. They won't. But this isn't because they're mean; if you think about the thousands of apps that get launched every week, the review sites would soon go bust if they tried to purchase even a small percentage just to review them - especially as a high number of those will turn out to be duds. Also, remember that many review sites are generally run by just a handful of people on a tight budget. So buying lots of apps is simply not appealing to them.

This means providing the sites with freebies. For example, if you're developing your app for Apple's platform you can supply the review sites with 'promo codes'. A promo code is a promotional aid provided by Apple that allows anyone to download your app from the App store for free. (You can request promo codes from within *iTunes Connect* on the Apple Developer website). To redeem a promo code, the user opens iTunes and clicks the 'Redeem' link. After typing in the special code, they are then able to download the app free of charge. Up until late in 2010, this feature was only available to iTunes users who had a US iTunes account, but it's now been expanded worldwide, and so any iTunes account holder in any country can use promo codes.

If you're developing for a different platform, determine if this type of promotional mechanism is available and use it.

Known issues

If you are aware of an issue in your app that you'll be fixing soon, absolutely, definitely tell the reviewer. You see, when a reviewer writes about an issue with your app, it can be given either a positive or negative slant – and this all depends on how the reviewer comes across the issue in the first place. For example, if the reviewer finds a bug in your app that you've been hoping he or she wouldn't have found, (and worse, that you haven't even documented or noted on your website), the chances are that the bug will be reported negatively in the review - the reviewer will want to show what he's found – all at the expense of your app sales. Put simply, it won't do your review any good and, depending on the severity, will possibly put off many potential buyers of your app.

However, if you inform the reviewer about the potential of the bug being found, (for example, when you dropped them that email with the promo code attached), the chances are that they will highlight it in their review, (as expected), but that they will also report that you are furiously working on a fix that will be available in a soon-to-be-released update ('cos that's what you also told them, right?).

Putting that positive spin on a negative issue can change the whole tone of the review and leave the readers thinking that you're a serious developer with plans in place to provide app updates and bug fixes, as opposed to a dev who's just pushed out a buggy app with little or no plans in place to fix those bugs anytime soon.

Use sparingly

Remember, though – this forewarning of app reviewers should be used sparingly and with care; if your app contains multiple bugs or 'showstoppers' that you believe you need to warn the reviewers about, then take a tip from me. Don't bother submitting it to them in the first place! If your app contains this many issues, then it's not ready for prime time yet and should not be available for purchase. You'll get bad reviews, bad feedback from customers and your sales will stall – all things that you want to avoid. Therefore, your priority should be to get back to work fixing those bugs and only put your app up for review when it's ready.

Detecting 'Review Mode'

Many moons ago (in the early nineties) I worked for a visionary called Alan Solomon. Alan created *Dr. Solomon's Anti-Virus Toolkit* which, at the time, ran under MS Dos and Windows 3.1 to protect a user's computer from viruses. The AVTK (as we affectionately called it) was a leader in the market place, constantly getting rave reviews from journalists and publications that tested it against our competitors. It was quite impressive the way we always had the best detection rates. I'll let you into a little secret; we weighted those reviews in our favour. But how?!? *Review Mode.*

For most users running the AVTK, the chances of them coming across a virus was pretty slim at the time. This was before the explosion of the internet, and so while boot sector viruses (like Form) were almost common, file viruses were actually quite rare. Unless you were a reviewer, of course, with access to hundreds of viruses to test with. So Alan decided to implement Review Mode into our product. The idea behind it was sound:

•   If, during a scan, we only find one or two viruses then the chances are that the product is running on a 'normal' end user's computer. Therefore, run normally and find viruses in the normal way.

•   If, during a scan, we find hundreds of viruses then chances are that the product is being tested by a reviewer. Therefore, scan in 'grunt' mode where we are extra careful to scan things and areas that normally won't be infected. Because the reviewers were sneaky and would do non-standard things with files in order to out-fox the anti-virus, they would be surprised that the AVTK would still be able to find these infections when the other products failed. The result? Fantastic reviews.

If your app lends itself to being run in a similar way, why not explore the possibility of adding a Review Mode? It's not cheating, it's just giving the reviewer exactly what he wants.

Make allies

As with most things in life, if you have good allies, you'll find it easier to achieve your goals. The same applies to getting the word out about your app. If a review site has given your app a write-up, follow up on that by contacting the reviewer to thank them and also to provide them with updates, feedback or corrections - they'll appreciate it. Take the opportunity to start building relationships with these individuals, as you'll then find it easier to get column inches when you update your app (or ship a completely new one) later on down the road and want further coverage.

Why not try persuading the website to give away copies of your app by providing them with additional promo codes? The website benefits as they have freebies they can give away to their visitors, the visitors benefit as a number of them will be able to get their hands on free apps, and you'll benefit from the increased buzz around your app. More importantly, though, you'll continue to build that relationship with the review site, making them more receptive to you when you contact them in the future.

Paid reviews
Some review sites charge money in order to write and publish a review for your app. Whether or not this is worth it depends on the type and popularity of the site, so if you decide to go down this route make sure you do your research. Personally, I avoided these types of sites, but your mileage may vary. Also, remember that even though you pay someone to review your app, the review they produce may not be to your liking.

Guerrilla Marketing
When you look around, smartphones are everywhere to be seen nowadays. When I travel on the London Underground, I see numerous people poking, stroking and prodding their iOS, or Android handsets. When I'm down the West End, I see the same thing. When I go to the theatre with my wife, the amount of iOS devices on show is amazing. And what was even more amazing was the realisation that if I could only get each of these people to spend just a couple of quid on my app, I'd be made. But how was I going to do it? While the Elevator Pitch was something that I use in many situations, it's not always the right tool for the job. I needed something subtler, equally persuasive and something that didn't cost an arm and a leg.

And so I chose an online printer who would create 250 business cards to my design for under £5. Now that was a result! These business cards didn't have my name and contact details printed on them like traditional business cards, though - they simply had a screenshot of my app taking up one entire side of the card, and the other side contained my app's tag line, the 'App store' logo and the URL to my app in iTunes: www.itunes.com/apps/top-tens.

Now - I am armed! I always keep these cards with me and, whenever I see someone using an iPhone, I give them the card and a smile. Sometimes I accompany it with a condensed version of my Elevator Pitch, but more often than not, a quick "Check out this app, its great!" is more than enough. It works for me, and it will work for you, too. And did I mention it's cheap?

Another form of guerrilla marketing I employed was using any available computer to show my app.

NOTE: I'm not advising you to do this - an Apple employee suggested I leave their Oxford Street store when he caught me doing this recently!

Essentially, I would enter the store and browse for a bit then I would move on to the iPhone/iPod touch displays and load *every one* of them at my app's page on the App store. Also, on any available computers I would load up my app's website. My idea behind this was simple; get as many eyeballs on my app as possible. Even if only a small percentage of potential users see and read the app description, then that's got to be a good thing, right?

Be creative!
Even though I had managed to get a couple of review sites to produce good write-ups about Top-Tens, it still wasn't selling as much as I'd hoped. I got to thinking about different ways in which I could stimulate sales. During a particularly creative brainstorming session, I came up with what I thought was a humdinger: Sell my app (the whole kit and caboodle) on eBay!
My reasoning was thus:

• To get people/websites talking about my app, I had to do something that had never been done before.

• Stories of unusual items being sold on eBay typically generate a lot of interest.

- I could put Top-Tens up for sale, but with a high reserve price of £8,000.

- Chances are, the reserve price would not be met, but the interest might spark a mini sales boom on iTunes.
- If a bidding war ensued, it might generate headline coverage.

- If the reserve price were met, I'd sell it anyway.

When I come to a decision, I like to act – I'm not one for procrastination – and so less than 24 hours later, I put everything up for sale (source code, images, documentation, the lot) with the intention of selling the lot if the reserve price was met or, alternatively, keeping it if the reserve was not met and benefiting from the increase in sales. I think that's called a *win-win situation.*

From Macworld to the Wall Street Journal

Now the app was up for sale on eBay and so I had to start the marketing ball rolling without delay; pretty much immediately, I started sending out notifications to the various 'techy' websites and, as I calculated, they were interested!

I had feedback from a number of websites who I had made allies of through my previous marketing endeavours, and they were interested in running the story. I provided feedback and answered their queries. The following morning, a host of websites had run the "iPhone developer sells app on eBay" story and so interest was starting to build. And the auction views were going through the roof!

Then, I had an email from the Yukari Kane of the Wall Street Journal; she wanted to telephone-interview me, as they wanted to run the story, too! Things were definitely looking up, and I was beginning to see firsthand how clever marketing could really get that ball rolling. All I needed now to top things off was a bidding war!

And lo and behold, a bidding war did ensue; after the Wall Street Journal story was printed, the eBay listing got picked up and reported on by more and more news outlets, resulting in bid after bid after bid. However after almost 100 bids, the auction ended at £5200 – quite a way below my reserve price of £8000 and so, after the excitement and frenzy of the days after the app was posted, the app didn't sell on eBay after all.

However, as expected, I did benefit from increased sales due to the additional publicity of being the first iPhone app to go up for sale in this way. The app started working its way back up the sales charts, turning sales of tens of units per day into sales of hundreds of units – proving that a clever and innovative marketing idea can boost sales enormously if executed correctly.

When it comes to marketing, then, sit down, put your creative hat on and thrash out some of those 'off the wall' ideas. One of them could just be the thing that captures the attention of the media and drives your app to the top of the sales charts.

Traditional app Marketing techniques

My flirtation with eBay mentioned above is one example of thinking outside of the box. However, while this type of attention grabbing technique is useful, you mustn't neglect the traditional marketing techniques that will help you to sell your app. These include:

- Online advertising
- Print media advertising
- T-Shirts, key rings, etc.

These are all effective and proven methods of marketing - however, like most things, they will only yield results if approached in the correct way. In addition, these forms of marketing tend to consume money. Which brings me on to...

Budgets

You didn't think you could get away with marketing for free did you? Sure – if you're canny enough you can kick start a campaign with little, or no, money. But to make an impact, to put into place a really effective campaign, you'll need to spend some money. And that means working out a budget. Even developers who realise the importance of providing a marketing budget will end up under-specifying it, but the important thing to realise is that if you want to make money, you have to spend money. And while that may be a bitter pill to swallow for many, remember that no medicine tastes nice.

A good starting place is trying to put aside around 10-15% of your revenue in order to pay for your marketing endeavours. This may sound like a lot, but in reality its not. Just remember that spending on your marketing is necessary and, unfortunately, unavoidable.

Review it

Its important realise that, whatever marketing plan you decide on, it is not fixed in stone. By their very nature, marketing plans should be fluid and flexible - allowing for tweaks and amendments along the way. Keep a close eye on your marketing efforts, not only at the start of your campaign but throughout its duration. If your goals or targets are not being met, review your campaign and revise it accordingly.

As a matter of course, your plan should be reviewed at least once a quarter and if things aren't working out don't be afraid to make changes.

Featured App

Getting mentioned in an App store is something to really aspire to. For example, Apple's App store has Staff Picks and New and Noteworthy sections which highlight an app to extremely large numbers of users. Getting your app in one of these categories is the Holy Grail of app writers like you and me. If your app gets mentioned (read: promoted) by Apple in this way, then you're pretty much golden - typically, you'll get thousands of hits per day while your app is featured.

But how do you get featured?

Well, nobody outside of Apple actually knows how they decide which apps are featured or not; Apple has an in-house team that identifies apps worthy of being featured and, in true Apple style; this is done under extreme secrecy. This team then contacts the developer and requests additional collateral that can be used on the special page Apple will add to iTunes to promote the app. For example, you may be asked to provide more artwork or more expansive copy.

While you'll find it impossible to influence Apple directly, (for example by emailing them and asking to be featured), clever marketing *outside* of the App store may draw their attention to your app which, subsequently, may result in it being featured.

Don't set the wrong price

The iPhone app market is extremely price sensitive. However, try to avoid the 'race to the bottom' scenario that took over the store shortly after it when live. The race to the bottom is the phenomenon where app developers feel they need to charge the lowest price possible for their app as they don't believe it will sell for anything more. This means we end up with many apps being sold for 59p when, in reality, they are worth much more than that.

The problem is that users have become familiar with this type of pricing and so even though your app may be worth every penny of its £9.99, you'll struggle to find any buyers.

Don't forget the free version

While it's always good to charge for an app, remember that 'free' is also good. A free version is another important part of your arsenal. Free versions of your app give your users a tantalizing taste of what your app can do, while dangling just enough for them to bite and purchase the full version. Weighing up what the free version can give to your potential customers is not easy, though. You'll need to strike a balance between not giving away too much that your customer has no more need to purchase the full version, and not giving away too little – you want to entice your customers to 'Buy Now' after all!

For Top-Tens I decided to do a free version that would only show the top 3 items in any list instead of the complete top 10. This seems to be a good compromise for me as both the free and full versions of my app have healthy downloads.

The Bottom Line:

Your marketing efforts are key to the successful launch and longevity of your app. Pay careful attention to how your strategy is performing, and don't be afraid to junk unsuccessful campaigns and start again. Be creative and, ultimately, you will be rewarded.

LESSON 9: WHO NEEDS SOCIAL NETWORKS?

"I don't care what my old schoolmates are doing now. I don't want to know what my ex had for lunch. And why would I want to see pictures of my workmate taking her dog for a walk in the local park? (OK - maybe I would want to see that - but that's beside the point). Social networks are for sad people who don't have lives! So why should I need to think about accommodating them with my app? I'm not convinced."

In our previous lesson about marketing you may have wondered why we didn't mention social networking. That's because marketing via social networks deserves a lesson all of its own. Social networking is a powerful thing. When things go 'viral' on the Internet, nine times out of ten there's a social network helping to spread it.

If you're on Facebook, Twitter, MySpace, LinkedIn, StumbleUpon, Bebo or one of the many, many other networks, then you will have seen things go viral already. Heck, you probably helped it along the way by clicking those 'like', 'share', or 'tweet' buttons that have become so popular on web pages over the last few years.

It's an easy and convenient way for individuals to help spread the word about interesting topics - so what's to stop you from using social networks in this way to help spread the news about your shiny new app?

It's interesting that various studies have shown that as social networking traffic has increased, visits to porn sites have decreased. A decade ago, porn-related searches carried out by 18 to 24 year olds accounted for 20% of all Internet searches made, however that figure has now dropped to under 10%. This shows that young people are spending much more of their time on social networking sites and so they simply don't have the time to visit adult sites any more.

It's undeniable that a vast audience awaits you. But you need to make sure you address that audience in the right way.

The Lay of the Land

Before you start formulating your first steps towards using social networks to promote your app, you need to understand the lay of the land. Are your competitors using social networks in order to promote their apps? If so, how would you rate their activities? Are they visible? And is their campaign engaging? What about the target audience for your app – are they social-network-savvy? If so, which networks do they use? Are *you* on those networks? For example, if you're creating a Twitter client, have you built up a large number of followers on Twitter who will help spread the news when you launch? I hope so! Because 20 followers just won't cut it.

Keep it real

One way to quickly turn people off is to obviously only be involved in the social network for marketing purposes. Remember, social networks are communities. So if you've gone to the trouble of creating an account, why not participate in the community? Share your knowledge about related subjects so that you don't come across as just a marketer. By being an active participant, you'll gain the respect of other members and you'll find spreading the word about you app much easier.

Bookmarking

You know that website for your app that we talked about previous lessons? Well – make sure that it contains Social Networking bookmarks and icons. This is a quick and easy way to get people to spread the word about your app.

The way it works is this:

1. The user finds his way onto your site – probably via a recommendation from a friend, by clicking the website link from your app's description page

on its App store, or maybe via a search carried out in their favourite search engine.

2. After digging around your site, the user decides that they like what they see. They then spot the Social Networking bookmarks that you've ever so carefully placed in the optimum positions on the each page.

3. As the user is a sociable person, they click the Facebook, LinkedIn, or whatever, icon to help spread the word to their friends and followers.

4. Goto1.

I use these icons to great effect on my websites. Depending on the type you use, you can even get regular reports which show how many clicks and recommendations others have made

Tactics

Depending on the social network you're attempting to market to, your tactics will vary but essentially will consist of you being active and visible in a consistent way. Facebook is, of course, the major one. To do things correctly, you need a Facebook following whom you can give frequent updates to. As well as your personal Facebook page, create a Facebook Fan page for your app, and link this prominently on your app's website and on its App store description page. Your objective here is to drive as much traffic as possible to your fan page and get people to 'Like' it so that others in their network are aware of it. You may also find it beneficial to use Facebook apps like Six Degrees which enable you see how your network is growing and also enables you to link to others outside of your immediate network.

Similarly with Twitter, frequent and interesting posts are the way to go. Remember to pace yourself, too; I've seen many would-be marketers burst onto the Twitter scene with a flurry of updates on day one, slightly less on days two and three, etc. and at the end of the month, their activity is almost non-existent and any of the followers they probably gained will be seriously considering hitting that 'un-follow' button.

When using Twitter or other types of services where you're posting frequent updates, above all remember to be professional at all times. It's cool to introduce a bit of humour to your posts once and again, but generally try to keep on message with every post you make – even the humorous ones.

Big Business

If you're ever in any doubt about the effectiveness of something like Twitter as a marketing tool, consider that all of the following big name brands are actively marketing their wares through Twitter: Dell, Starbucks, JetBlue, Comcast, The Home Depot, Southwest Airlines, Best Buy, Forrester Research, McAfee, Ford, Samsung, and Kodak. They can't all be wrong, right? Even celebrities have taken Twitter to their hearts and use it as their marketing machine of choice. And why not? It allows them to communicate with hundreds of thousands of their fans directly on their smartphones or other devices in real time.

Videos

Videos spread really well on social networking sites, and so this is something you should do to help promote your app. And if you do make a video, make it funny. Remember, people like to laugh – so a video that genuinely makes people laugh has a much better chance of going viral than one that doesn't. In fact, any video that triggers strong emotions in its viewers will stand a chance of becoming viral.

For Top-Tens, I created a spoof of Apple's "there's and app for that" series of ads. As Top- Tens highlights different top 10s in different Categories (such as books, film, music, etc.) I thought I'd use the tagline "there's a cat for that". Now, I'm no filmmaker, but I found that working with Apple's iMovie was a fantastic experience that allowed me to piece together a video that actually worked quite well. I'm not expecting Oscar nominations from it, but in terms of if showing prospective users what my app can do and how it works, I was very happy with the end result.

I then posted the video on YouTube and Vimeo and, again, linked them to my app's website, Facebook fan pages, etc.

The Key

When it comes to social networks, the key is to attack from all fronts. Don't think that just because you have a Facebook page which you update every couple of days, you've done everything you need to do. Because you haven't.

You'll need to complement all of your online activities and co-ordinate them with a social network slant. Ensure that everything is interlinked, so that the videos you mention in your posts are linked to your App store pages, and that your App store pages link to your website, which in turn links to favourable reviews, etc. Get the idea?

The Bottom Line:
Social networks cannot be ignored. While many individuals do use them to while away the hours, they can also be used for solid marketing activities. The trick is to make sure you've identified the right networks. Then, be consistent with your message and, above all, be you!

LESSON 10: WHO NEEDS DEVELOPERS?

"Believe me, I've tried but I just can't get my head around this programming lark. View Controllers, app delegates, provisioning profiles... it's a nightmare. So I'm hiring a developer to do the work for me. And this one is really cheap! Less than half the price of most of the others I've seen. And he says he'll get it all done by next week, too!"

Many aspiring app developers will reach the stage when the enormity of the task that they've undertaken becomes apparent. For some, this realisation will be on the very first day as they struggle to even get the SDK installed, for others it will come six months down the line when they come to a grinding halt after many late night sessions. And for others it will be somewhere in between.

So when this happens, what do you do? You plainly can't take the project any further yourself, so the two choices you have available to you are:

a) Cut your losses and jack the whole thing in
b) Hire a developer

For the purposes of this book, let's assume that the first option is not really an option. So hire a developer it is, then!

But how?

It's easy, really. You see, developers are an extremely resourceful bunch with supreme chameleonic tendencies that allow them to adapt as necessary to market forces and demands. In other words, if there's a demand, they'll fill it. And so with apps being the topic of the moment, an entire cottage industry has, unsurprisingly, sprung up around programmers offering to develop your app for you. For a fee, of course.

This is a good alternative for someone who has given up trying to develop an app because they've found it too difficult, or for someone who doesn't have programming skills, and so didn't even attempt to venture down the development road, but who still has an idea for an app that they want to bring to market.

Choose your developer wisely, though; making the wrong choice could be the difference between a bug-ridden app that languishes at the bottom of all sales and popularity charts, and a successful app that doesn't. As the saying goes: *your mileage may vary.*

Cold, hard, cash

The vast majority of developers will not be interested in "I've got an idea for a unique app, but I can't afford to pay you. Could you develop the app and then I'll give you a share of the profits?"

The reason they won't be interested in that type of deal is because they know how difficult it is to eke out a profit from an app. Especially when that profit has to be split between two parties. Granted, if an app is a mega-successful, then a deal like this would likely pay back the developer many times over what he would have charged to develop the app. However, the majority of apps aren't mega-successful - and so the developer knows that he is more likely to lose out if he proceeds in this way.

For this reason, when you approach a developer with that type of deal, you're likely to get a big fat "Thanks, but no thanks". He or she will do the work for you, but they'll only want to deal in cold, hard, cash. Or a wire transfer, where available.

Finding a developer

There's no denying the fact that developing mobile apps is now big business - and, as with all big businesses, there are trustworthy, diligent and capable individuals who will do a great job for you, as well as less capable, less diligent, and less trustworthy individuals who won't. Your task is to sort the wheat from the chaff and identify, and engage with, the former, while avoiding the latter at all costs.

A number of websites have sprung up recently where developers can ply their trade to anyone looking. Essentially, the developers list their competencies and, preferably, their experience on the site while potential customers pitch their app ideas. The developers quote for the projects that interest them and, eventually, the customer decides who to go with.

To protect both sides, payment on sites like these is normal done via an 'escrow' method where you first pay the money to a secure third party account that the developer does not have access to. This way, the developer can't take your money and run. Also, it provides the developer with security and a carrot; he knows that the money is there waiting for him and that it will only be released when he's finished the project to specification. Sites like these make it extremely easy to find a developer for your app.

Choosing a developer
If you plan on using this type of service, ensure that you do your homework before parting with your hard-earned cash. The saying goes that a fool and his money are easily parted. As you're reading this book, you're obviously no fool - and so this won't apply to you. However, ensure that you fully detail and specify your app if you are looking for accurate and realistic quotes. Failure to do so will result in confusion on both ends and the potential of you choosing the wrong developer for the job.

Most developers will want to show you what they're capable of and will have a portfolio of at least 3 or 4 completed apps that they can show you. It's worthwhile downloading these apps (especially if they're free) so that you can get a feel for what the developer can produce. If a developer does not have a portfolio, avoid him. Yes, he may be able to give you a rock-bottom price, but chances are any app he produces for you will generate rock-bottom sales. This is a generalisation, of course, because every developer has to start somewhere. But if he can't show you a commercial app that he has produced, alarm bells should definitely start ringing.

References

So, your developer has proudly shown you his portfolio containing apps that he says he's written for many satisfied customers. He hasn't provided the cheapest quote, but is reasonably priced. He's responsive to your email requests and seems to know what he's talking about. Should you go for him? Well, before you take the plunge ask him if he'd mind you speaking to some of his past customers. Ask him if he'd mind you asking them for a reference.

If the developer doesn't want this then, again, alarm bells should start ringing. In most instances, though, the developer will be happy for you to speak to his past customers. When you do, state the facts: you're thinking of hiring this individual to write an app for you, and you would like to find out how well he worked with them while developing their app. Was he responsive? Did he keep them informed? Did he meet their deadlines? Did he produce what they wanted – or did he produce what *he* wanted?

Remember, at every stage of the process, you are in charge. You are the one with the money. You want the app written. You call the shots. If a developer doesn't seem to understand this, then kick 'em to the curb. There are lots more who are just as capable of producing your app for you.

The contract

Once you've settled on a developer, you need to draw up a contract. The contract is vitally important because it protects both you and the developer from fraud and other types of liabilities. A proper, legal contract is most desirable. This is because, if things do go pear- shaped and you end up in court, a badly written contract will be full of holes and simply not worth the paper it's written on.

There are many websites available from where you can download a contract template. These can be very useful as most of the hard work and loopholes will have already been covered, however if you decide on using one of these it's still advisable to run it past your lawyer or attorney.

However you decide to obtain your contract, some of the essential areas that it should cover are:

• **Payment** – specify the payment terms that the developer has agreed to. For example, half of the full cost up front, and the remainder when the project is complete.

• **Standards** – specify that the developer must adhere to the most commonly used and accepted standards while developing your app. Some companies (such as Apple) will reject your app if it's not written to the appropriate standards.

• **Warranties and Liabilities** – Who is liable if the app misbehaves while on customer's smartphones or tablets? Specify that the developer should agree to fix any major problems that come to light after the app has shipped, without any additional payment.

• **Credits** – Will the developer be credited in your app? Agree this now and, if possible, where in the app the credit will appear. A friend on mine had her app plastered with links to the developer's website, much to her chagrin simply because she agreed to the developer's verbal request to add a link, but didn't specify where it should be located.

• **Disputes** – it's worthwhile adding a section covering what happens if a dispute arises. Your priority should always be to address any disputes and resolve them amicably. This benefits both sides equally.

• **Cancellation** – Obviously, no-one wants the contract to reach this stage, but it's wise to cover this possibility. Having an easy way out of a contract is not always possible, but it will be considerably easier if your contract has a built-in 'get out' clause. So think about what happens if the agreement is cancelled before the project is complete, and ensure this is added to your contract.

Non-Disclosure Agreement
Remember when you joined your smartphone's developer program? The application process probably required you to agree to a Non-Disclosure Agreement (NDA) which stipulated, amongst other things, that you wouldn't blab about any confidential stuff that you may be privy to during your time enrolled in the program.

This is understandable - people (competitors) always want to know what large corporations are up to next, and if they can find out before the corporation wants them to find out, they can use that information to their commercial advantage by starting work on rival products or services early. For this reason, most NDAs prohibit this behaviour, threatening legal action for anyone who breaks it.

So why should you be any different? If you hire a developer to work on your app you'll be, effectively, giving him the keys to the castle; you'll be giving him access to your source code, your future plans, and many other things that you may not want to disclose or allow others to see. Therefore, you need to protect yourself in the same way that the larger corporations do - and that means getting together a proper, legal, NDA. This tells any developers that you sub- contract work to that you know what you're doing. It tells them that they should treat your project seriously and not disclose details about it to others without your prior written consent.

Remember, if you get your developer to sign an NDA it's a legally binding document, so make sure that it makes sense! Just like with the contracts, above, there are websites available that provide NDA templates and, in most situations, these will be good enough. If you can afford it, though, it might be worthwhile getting an NDA drawn up legally. This way, you're completely protected should anything go awry.

Garbage in, Garbage out
Don't expect your developer to perform miracles. You're in the driving seat with this project, so don't assume that just because you now have a developer on board, you can sit back, drink Pimms, and wait for the finished app to appear on an App store.

Ensure that you've *fully* specified in the contract what your app will do, and what your app won't do. Ensure that your developer *understands* this. Don't wait until the app is near complete before you scratch your head and inform the developer that the app he's produced bears no resemblance to the app you envisioned. In short, be fully involved in the development process.

Ask the developer to send you builds of your app on a regular basis. When you get these, thoroughly test them and report your findings back to the developer. Maybe you don't like the fonts being used, or the icons are the wrong size, or performing a combination of actions causes the app to crash. Its far better that you discover these issues at this stage, rather than right at the end of the process when your developer thinks that he's finished the job. Or worse, having your customers unearth them further on down the line. If you fail to provide solid guidance and input to your developer at this critical stage, I guarantee you won't be happy with the output.

The Bottom Line:
If you don't believe you can write and deliver your app yourself then rest assured, the right developer can do it for you. The trouble is, finding that developer is not an easy task. Care must be taken to select the right individual for the task. Lastly, when you have them, communication is the key; neglect this part of the relationship and your finished app won't resemble your envisioned app in the slightest.

GO FOR IT!

Well - there you have it.

I wrote this ebook with the intention that it would give you the ammunition that you need to embark on your app creation journey. When I started my own journey, I had no idea what to expect. I didn't realise that thorough research would have made things so much easier for me. I didn't understand the importance of creating an elevator pitch that would enable me to tell people about my app with ease and confidence.

I had no idea that I would have to provide customers with technical support, and thought social networks were only used by people who had too much time to kill.

I knew nothing about evaluating the competition to see how they approached, and overcame, issues, or how to make the most of *their* research to benefit *my* app.

I thought roadmaps were for project managers and couldn't see how they would fit in with my plans. And the list goes on.

To cut a long story short, I had a lot of misconceptions and made a lot of mistakes on my journey, and so I thought it would be cool to highlight some of these in an ebook so that others could learn from my missteps.

Hopefully, this ebook has given you the ammunition you need to start your journey with confidence. By following the advice given in the various chapters, I believe you'll be well on your way to writing a killer app and, hopefully, making some money from your efforts!.

So now that you've been armed, it's up to you to. Good Luck!

Rod.

ACKNOWLEDGEMENTS

This ebook would not have been possible without the input, support and assistance of many people.

I won't be able to mention everyone here, so I'll keep it brief. First and foremost, thank you to my beautiful wife, Yvonne. I'm sure you've heard the saying: *"Behind every great man, there's a woman"*. Well, in my case, it's: *"Behind the man, there's a great woman"*. How she puts up with me, I'll never know. Thank you to my troublesome, but lovable kids Lucas, Llywelyn, Trieve, and Indiana. How I put up with *them*, I'll never know. Thanks to my mum, Veronica for the guidance you've always provided.

Thanks Wayne, Bryan, the other Brian, Carl, Stuart, Kenny, Gemma, Mark, and Trevor for the help, advice, and friendship over the years – it's appreciated!

Last, but not least, thank you to Jonathan, Sjoerd, Kevin, Ashley, and Mick for the jokes that help the wheels go round (and the proofreading services).

ABOUT THE AUTHOR

Rod Cambridge is a computer security expert based in London, England. Rod has worked in the computer security industry for the last twenty years in a variety of positions, including technical support, development and technical writing, and has 4 granted US patents in his name in the area of computer security.

Rod has a passion for mobile computing, which started back in the eighties when he worked on a cutting-edge Electronic Point of Sale (EPoS) project based on Psion's handheld Organiser product for Marks and Spencer - a major UK retailer.

After Apple released their first Newton device in 1993, Rod entered a competition run by Apple UK to design an application or service for the fledgling device. While he didn't win, his NewtonPoint proposal came in at a very respectable second place - winning Rod the usage of a Mac for three months, together with all the development software he'd need to produce a proof-of-concept of his proposal.

NewtonPoint was a system that would provide the user with location-specific information beamed via infrared from strategically placed points (NewtonPoints) to their Newton. For example, the NewtonPoint at the entrance to a shopping mall would beam a map of the mall to the user's Newton, together with any special offers, etc. as the user entered the mall.

Due to the fact that the infrastructure required would be much too costly, (and risky), to implement, NewtonPoint didn't proceed any further after Rod completed the proof-of-concept of the client software. That this idea was proposed by Rod in the early nineties, however, shows his credentials as a visionary and forward-thinking individual; Way before GPS in handhelds was proposed, Rod saw the importance of location-specific services for handheld devices.

Jump forward to spring 2006 when Rod announced his innovative website expodition.com. Expodition provided users of Apple's iPod with another location-aware service by allowing them to type in a postcode (zip code) of the area they were travelling to, in order to receive a 'snapshot' of that area in a format that could be viewed on an iPod.

iPods of 2006 vintage were mainly text-based, and so the snapshots provided by Expodition were text files compiled on-the-fly by the PHP scripts running on the back-end of the website. In addition, these snapshots were personalized and tailored to each user based on the user's profile, which specified tastes such as favourite types of food, whether the user liked pubs, clubs, museums, etc.

The service provided by Expodition was groundbreaking - mainly because it gave iPods a new purpose for travelling users. Now, in addition to getting music and video from their iPods, users were also able to get detailed information about their intended destination.

Unfortunately for Rod, six months after Expodition went live, Apple announced the iPhone; with it's advanced OS and built-in support for location-awareness. This leap in technology had an adverse effect on the service provided by Expodition, witnessed by a steady decline in usage of the site after the iPhone shipped. In addition, when the iPod touch was introduced a few months later, it became obvious that Expodition would not be the success that Rod had hoped.

In 2009, Rod launched his first iPhone app, Top-Tens, which allows users to keep track of a number of top 10 lists, such as the top 10 books on Amazon.com or songs on iTunes. In total, almost 100 different top 10 lists can be tracked by the app and more will undoubtedly be added in the future.

Rod continues to innovate, and in 2010 launched appdebut.com a website that aims to help developers give their app a debut, while at the same time allowing users to find out about apps before they're released.

Contacting Rod

Rod would love to hear from you. Probably the easiest way to get in touch is via his website: www.appdebut.com. Any updates, downloads or errata that might be available for this ebook will be posted there.

This is Rod's first ebook – but hopefully will not be his last. Therefore, any feedback, both positive and negative, will be welcome. In addition, Rod will also do his best to reply to each comment as it's received although, due to volume, this may not always be possible.

You can email Rod directly at: rod@appdebut.com or follow him on Twitter @appdebut.

iPod, iPhone, iPad and their associated trademarks are copyright Apple Computer. Other trademarks mentioned in this ebook are copyright their respective owners.

CPSIA information can be obtained at www.ICGtesting.com
Printed in the USA
BVOW031219090911

270911BV00010B/80/P